TIMELESS Việt Nam

Photographs by Cảnh Tăng

Red Rock Press ▪ New York New York

COVER PHOTO
Launching the Net

Photographs copyright © 2013 Nguyễn Phước Cảnh Tăng
Foreword copyright © 2013 Peter Yarrow

ISBN: 978-1-9331-7640-6
Red Rock Press
New York New York
www.redrockpress.com

English translations of Vietnamese poetry in this book by Huỳnh Sanh Thông first appeared in *An
Anthology of Vietnamese Poems* (1996) and are used here with the permission of Yale University Press;
translations by John Balaban of folk-poetry lyrics initially appeared in *Ca Dao Việt Nam/Vietnam Folk
Poetry* (2003) and are used here with the permission of the translator; translations of folk-poetry lyrics
by Linh Dinh are used here with the permission of the translator. Additional research and translation
were provided by Dat P. Nguyen. Red Rock Press thanks all parties.

Design by Lori S. Malkin

Library of Congress Cataloging-in-Publication Data

Nguyen, Canh Tang 1959-
Timeless Vietnam / photographs by Canh Tang Phuoc Nguyen.
        p. cm.
  ISBN 978-1-933176-40-6
1. Vietnam--Pictorial works. 2. Vietnam--Social life and
customs--Pictorial works. I. Title.
DS556.39.T36 2012
959.700'2'2--dc23
                                2012018782

Printed in China

To my dear wife, Hiep

Open your eyes, admire your timeless land!

—from *The Bạch Đằng River*

Cảnh non sông xưa và nay mở đôi mắt mà xem thử!

—trích từ *Sông Bạch Đằng*

This book takes its title from the fifth line (above) of a treasured poem written by the 14th-century Vietnamese emperor Trần Minh Tông. The poem may be found in Vietnamese and in English on page 139.

Timeless River ▼

imeless Vietnam is an astonishingly beautiful exposition of the way of life of the people of Vietnam. It includes some scenes similar to ones I glimpsed during my first visit to Vietnam, and many others that eluded me. It strikes me as a work of authenticity, as could only have been captured by a talented Vietnamese photographer.

I'd come to Vietnam in 2005 hoping to resolve questions that had haunted me since my participation in the antiwar movement of the 1960s and '70s. I needed to know if my decade-long effort made sense in the light of what Vietnam had become.

I'd opposed the United States' involvement in what can be viewed either as a civil war or Vietnam's war of liberation from control by a Western power. The United States, in my opinion, had no right to intervene in this internal struggle in Vietnam and, worse, it had installed a puppet leadership in Saigon that did not, as I saw it, represent the hearts of the Vietnamese people. The North Vietnamese government in Hanoi was Communist but sought to pursue the aspirations of the people: It was fighting to prevent Vietnam from being colonized, as it had been for most of the previous 1,200 years, and was seeking to reunify this ancient and heroically unbowed nation.

As an antiwar activist I'd co-organized a march on Washington in 1969 attended by half a million people and I'd engaged many of my fellow performers in public efforts to oppose the war. As a member of the folk trio, Peter, Paul and Mary, I was proud to sing songs such as *If I Had a Hammer* and Bob Dylan's

Blowing In The Wind. When we sang Pete Seeger's "Where have all the flowers gone . . . where have all the young men gone?", we were singing not only of the pointless deaths of what became 57,000 American soldiers, but also of the Vietnamese soldiers and civilian men, women and children who were dying daily. The Vietnamese ultimately lost two and a half-million people including male noncombatants, women and children.

My 2005 trip was sponsored by the Fund for Reconciliation and Development, a non-profit that had worked for 25 years to bring about healing cultural, economic and political exchanges between the people of Vietnam and the United States. During my visit, I attended meetings around the issue of Agent Orange and its ghastly legacy of three generations of birth defects. I also had time to walk the streets of Ho Chi Minh City (once Saigon), Huế and Hanoi, dodging their eager hordes of cyclists careening in all directions. I visited markets where fish, vegetables, exotic foods and crafts were sold. Though I was clearly an American, easily identified by the way I dressed, I encountered no hostility. The Vietnamese people were warm and welcoming.

I also had important questions for which I needed to find answers. The answer to one of them was: No. The people of Vietnam bear no anger towards the people of America.

The Vietnamese attribute American destructiveness of the war years to the U.S. leadership at the time, not to its people. In the same way, the Vietnamese bear no grudge toward the French who'd colonized them for nearly a century, or the Chinese who'd earlier occupied Vietnam for most of a thousand years.

Timeless Vietnam shows the way of life of the people of Vietnam. It is a work about common folk, some of whom create works of art or participate in age-old rituals. The photos make art of the patterns of rice paddies and the men and women who farm them, the nets cast by fishermen, and even of stones waiting to be placed in a new road and the women who gather them. We also sense the rhythm of work by meticulous creators of straw hats and we sense the pride in the craft of a young man fashioning a traditional metal necklace.

These works, all of them, are celebrations of the beauty and the spirit that have nurtured and sustained the people of Vietnam in times of painful struggle, in times of peace, in times of sorrow or joy.

In the old folk verses or other short poems in *Timeless Vietnam* that comment on and enhance the subject matter of the photographs, one can sense the underpinnings of Vietnam's national culture. There is humor along with simple human grace, deep appreciation and love of country and a fierce commitment to preserving heritage. These poems are new to me but now I think it was not the politicians but the poets who could have told any war-minded nation—the Chinese, the French, the Americans—that the Vietnamese would successfully defy those who would threaten to take over their beloved country.

Cảnh Tăng's photographs let us experience the sweet wonderment of children gazing at a curtain of tiny, paper cranes (symbols of good luck). They let us share the exuberance of a wedding party. They show us, too, the generations together, the elders' faces etched in timeless wisdom and strength possessed only by grandmothers and grandfathers—they who have seen so much and who have not only survived but thrived in spite of overwhelming odds.

To me, the images speak volumes. I imagine the people who populate the photographer's world saying: *Look around you. See our ancient ways that respect the beauty and bounty of our land and rivers. See what is truly meaningful in our lives. The fields of rice and the rhythms of the sun, the moon and the tide lend us the strength to endure adversity and to heighten the joy we find in the company of one another.*

I left Vietnam convinced that I'd been right to oppose the war, not only because today the U.S. and Vietnam are great friends (and we are Vietnam's largest trading partner) but also because I was touched by a wisdom that transcended my Western perspective. That wisdom challenged the notion that a nation (or its people) could ever simply be either right or wrong. That wisdom encompassed forgiveness and trust in the capacity for goodness inherent in the human spirit.

I think you can sense this wisdom in the images before you of a beautiful land and its people. Your time spent wandering through the pages of *Timeless Vietnam* will be the next best thing to journeying there yourself.

Enjoy this amazing book, and know that I will be watching your smiles from afar, imagining your eyes brightening as you explore the beauty and spirit of Vietnam and the heart of its people.

—Peter Yarrow

Rescuing the Rice ▼

PART ONE

THIS LAND THAT BREATHES

Buffalo, let me tell you something
Go out and plow with me,
Out in the field, be a farmer.
Me here, you there—who's griping?
As long as the rice stalks are blooming,
There will be blades of grass for you to eat.

—from ca dao (folk poems), translated by Linh Dinh

This verse can be found in Vietnamese on page 140.

Heading Home ▼

◀ Rescuing the Rice 2

I've often suffered much in summer heat—
my skin, all dried and shriveled up, has cracked.
I've often gone through hell in rains and floods—
They've riddled me with sores, torn me to shreds.

I share the happiness of village folks
when they bring in good crops, their cares and woes
when harvests fail. I even feel the thrills
of country boys and girls at their love trysts.

So gloom and tedium haunt my life no more.
In my poor village, well content I stay.
With rapture I absorb through all my pores
Aromas exhaled from the fields, the earth.

—from *The Country Road* by Tế Hanh, translated by Huỳnh Sanh Thông

This excerpt can be found in Vietnamese on page 140.

Pulling ▶

Pitching the Rice ▶

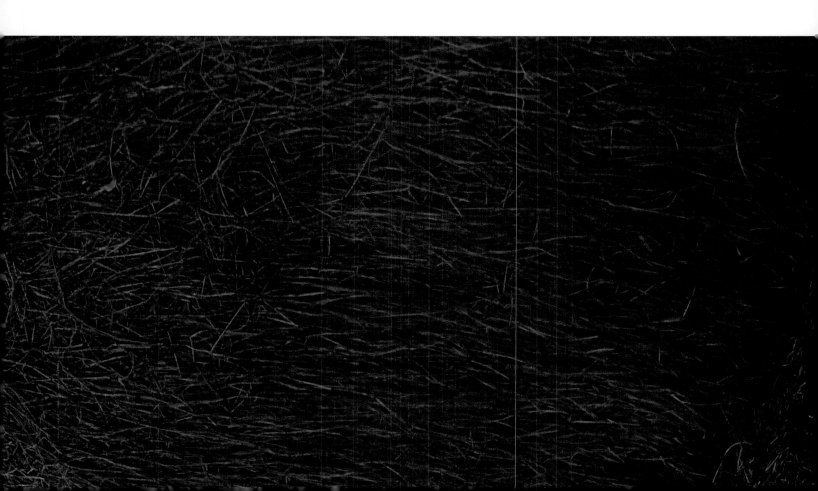

▲ Hué Noodles

Mr. Moon, Mr. Moon
Come down and hang out with me.
There's white rice in the pot,
And sticky rice in the pot,
Square rice cakes with bean paste,
A jug of wine and a straw mat,
A boy scooping for oysters, and a girl
Holding a baby. We can go watch the fishermen trawl.
There's a coconut-shell dipper in the water jar,
And a weaved basket for rinsing rice.
There's a comb for your hair,
Water buffalo working the rice paddies,
Water spinach in the pond, Mr. Star in the sky.

—from *ca dao*, translated by Linh Dinh

This verse can be found in Vietnamese on page 141.

PART TWO

FROM THE WATERS

Filling the Net ▶

Waiting for Fresh Fish ▶

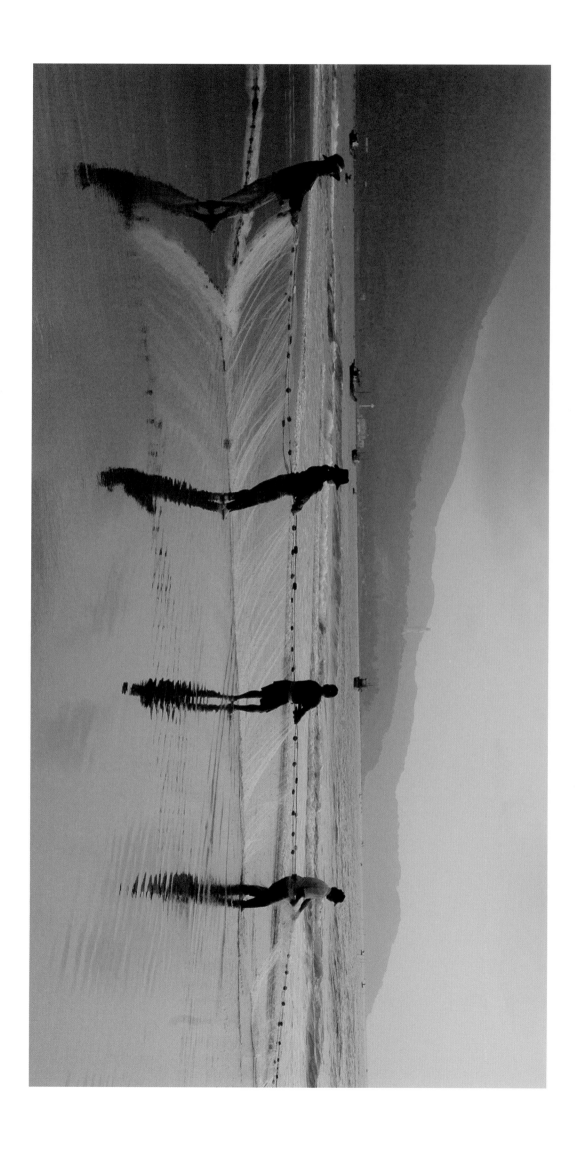

Breakfast on the River ▶

Inspection 2 ▲

Inspection 1 ▲

Throwing the Net

◀ *Lookout*

The Fisherman Speaks

Beyond harm's reach persist in your own sphere—

some stream or sea none covets or disputes.

Plying a paddle, row your river boat

and catch a livelihood from dawn to dusk.

Weave your way through rivers' zigs and zags,

with fishing line and rod made of bamboo.

Befriend the moon by night, the wind by day—

sing a gay tune, enjoy a jar of wine.

Drift past where cranes resort, where oysters haunt.

In nature take delight, at ease and free,

The fish and shrimp, by Heaven sent, abound.

You eat your fill—for what else could you wish?

—from *Dương Từ Hà Mậu* by Nguyễn Đình Chiểu,
translated by Huỳnh Sanh Thông

This excerpt can be found in Vietnamese on page 141.

▼ *Pole Fishing*

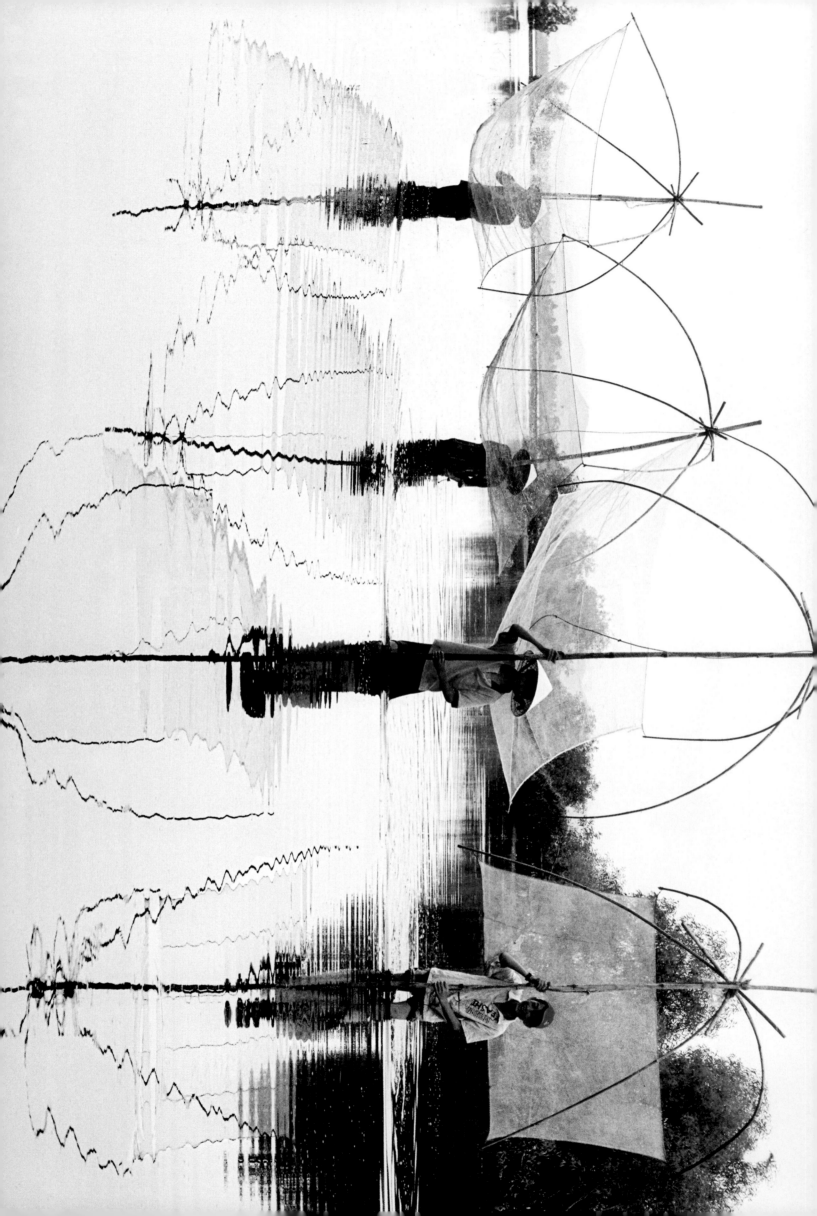

◄ Net Nuances

▼ Mother Net

▲ *House of Sand*

60

Clean-up

▼

▼ *Through the Breakers*

Venturing Out

Each evening, ducks paddle, egrets fly.
Mister Elephant snaps sugarcane then strides into the forest.
I'll follow to strip rattan for plaits,
fetching them home to make a sling for you to go peddling.
Selling at no loss? Why, that's a profit.
Go on, have a look at the sun's face, at the moon's.

—from ca dao, translated by John Balaban
This excerpt can be found in Vietnamese on page 142.

◄ *Riding Home*

Fence on Vĩnh Hiền ◄

The Road to Huế

The road to Huế twists around and around
Verdant mountains, aquamarine water, like a quaint painting.
Loving you, I would cross all the distance
Facing hidden risks in Truông Nhà Hồ and Tam Giang Lagoon.

—from ca dao, translated by Dat P. Nguyen
This excerpt can be found in Vietnamese on page 142.

Crossing the Tam Giang Lagoon ▼

◀ *Golden Net 2*

Golden Net 3 ▶

For Two Voices

Man

A river so vast, a fish will disappear.
If we are meant to be together, I can wait a thousand years.

Woman

Repair the dike if it's your paddy.
If it's meant to be, we'll be together. Don't bother waiting.

—from ca dao, translated by Linh Dinh

This excerpt can be found in Vietnamese on page 142.

Sunset on Lập An Lagoon ▼

Part Three

From the Hands of Artisans

Young Carver

▲ *Statues of Gods*

At the Forge ▼

In Praise of the Hat

It's round, full round, yet not a hollow thing.
It shelters and promotes on all four sides.
Left there, it looks like a parasol;
Once on, it will defy both sun and rain.
It covers every head and favors none;
from dawn to dark it staunchly serves the chief.
Aloft it sits, positioned at the top:
a grateful world takes refuge underneath.

—translated by Huỳnh Sanh Thông

This poem can be found in Vietnamese on page 142.

Mary Hats ▼

Shelter from the Sun
▼

◀ *Three Generations*   *In Balance* ▶

▲ Street Vendors

Fan Maker ▼

▲ *Ring of Life*

Village Artist ▼

▲ *Ceramicist*

Ode to the Sewing Needle

Well-tempered, it stays straight and will not warp:
don't try to bend it into some vile hook.
With skill it interweaves five hues of thread;
to beauty it can add four seasons' flowers.

—from the 15th-century *Hồng Đức Anthology*,
translated by Huỳnh Sanh Thông

This excerpt can be found in Vietnamese on page 143.

▼ *Embroidery Circle*

Weavers
▼

Flowers in Water

▼

▲ *Clean Start*

Street-side Selling ▼

◀ Burning Boots

Ancestral Altar ▶

◀ The Wrestlers

▼ *Here Come the Bride and Groom*

Offering Betel

A whole areca nut and a fresh betel bit
Here, Xuân Hương has lime-pasted it.
If our love is true, marry them red
Green leaf, or white lime (alone), won't make it.

—by Hồ Xuân Hương, translated by Dat P. Nguyen

This poem can be found in Vietnamese on page 143.

▲ *Festive Table*

▼ *Hand in Hand*

Lanterns on Pagoda Steps ▲

Lanterns Afloat ▼

Canopy
▼

The Hibiscus

The water gleams and mirrors this red flower.
It bears no stain, for Buddha is its Heart.
At break of day it blooms, by dusk it falls.
O wondrous law! A thing becomes no-thing.

—by Nguyễn Trãi, translated by Huỳnh Sanh Thông

This poem can be found in Vietnamese on page 143.

◀ Hibiscus in the Morning

Red Lanterns in Autumn ▶

▲ *Painting the Đầu Lân*

Lion Dance ▼

▼ *Splash, Splash*

Farewell Song

On high, the moon must wax and wane by turns—
down here, how can we humans shun hard times?
A man will take what happens with due calm—
when in distress, he will confront distress.
Heaven has eyes to watch our road ahead—
now exiled, we shall someday yet come home.
After these years, we all shall still be young.
Here flows the river Đà, there stands Mount Ấn.
Our land is waiting—we shall deck it out.
Now we must part, but shall join hands again.
That gaffer lost his horse—was it bad luck?
Tomorrow, as the Maker will arrange,
we shall return from all four seas and meet.
Within this world there must be room for us.
The hills may fall, the seas may rise;
the sky may tilt, the earth may heave—
our hearts of stone and iron shall stay true.
The moon that's waning shall wax full again.

—by Huỳnh Thúc Kháng, translated by Huỳnh Sanh Thông

This poem can be found in Vietnamese on page 144.

Grandmother and Granddaughter ▶

▶ *Wishing 2*

About the Photographs

COVER

TITLE QUOTE

LAUNCHING THE NET

Lộc An Lagoon, Lăng Cô Town, Thừa Thiên-Huế, May, 2010

TIMELESS RIVER

The Bạch Đằng River today reflects much of yesterday, April, 2012.

PART ONE This Land that Breathes

RESCUING THE RICE 1

A flooded field in Hương Thủy, Thừa Thiên-Huế, September, 2009

A NEW DAY

A farmer takes his buffalo to feed on wild grass before their work begins, Quảng Điền District, Thừa Thiên-Huế, March, 2010.

MUD PADDY

A farmer guides plow-pulling buffalo during the wet season, Mong A town, Phú Mỹ, Phú Vang, Thừa Thiên-Huế, 2012.

HEADING HOME

Mother and daughter lead a buffalo from a rice paddy, Hà Giang, 2009.

DAY IS DONE

Back to pasture, Hà Giang, 2009

RESCUING THE RICE 2

Gathering the swamped rice grass, Hương Thủy, Thừa Thiên-Huế, September, 2009

RICE ROUTE

Women load boat with their harvest to float it home from the paddy, An Truyền, 2009.

CHORUS OF THE SEASON 1

It's a long walk from the rice fields to the road in the commune of Thủy Thanh, Phú Vang, Thiên-Huế, September, 2009.

CHORUS OF THE SEASON 2

The farmers' bamboo yokes seem heavier as they walk atop a dike separating their fields from a river, Phú Vang, Thiên-Huế, September, 2009.

MIRACLE OF STEAM HEAT

A family spreads a rice-flour mixture on fabric covering a steaming pot, one of several steps to rice crackers or spring-roll wrappers, An Truyền, Phú An, Phú Vang, Thừa Thiên–Huế, 1998.

WELCOME SUNSHINE 1

A young woman hangs thin, rice-paper discs to dry, An Truyền, Phú An, Phú Vang, Thừa Thiên–Huế, 1998.

WELCOME SUNSHINE 2

Edible rice paper drying on the racks is destined to wrap shredded, fish-sauced delicacies, Thanh Hóa, 2010.

FLAVORS OF THE NEW YEAR

In the family yard, a mother and grandmother prepare banana-leaf wrapped rolls (*bánh tét*) for Tết, An Truyền, December, 2000.

GOING HOME

After the corn harvest, a H'mong woman hauls stalks to heat her home on a high plateau, Hà Giang, 2009.

MOUNTAIN HAUL

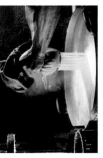

This mountain woman carries home from the market a bucket for rainwater. Her trip might be as long as 15 miles, Hà Giang, 2009.

ONTO THE COUNTRY ROAD

Earth fills the holes in this rocky path in the commune of Thủy Thanh, Phú Vang, Thừa Thiên Huế, 2009.

PULLING

A boy leads a bull pulling a rice-laden cart to the threshing floor, Quảng Điền, Thừa Thiên–Huế, 2008.

PITCHING THE RICE

Rice hay is used for cooking fuel, chicken coops and mushroom shelters, Quảng Điền, Thừa Thiên–Huế, 2008.

MUSHROOM HOUSES

Mushrooms grow in these suburban thatched structures, Thủy Lương, Phú Vang, Thừa Thiên–Huế, 2008.

UNDER THE SUN

Raking the sun-dried rice; sunshine keeps kernels intended for the bowl from germinating, Thủy Phủ, Hương Thủy, Thừa Thiên–Huế, 2009.

HUẾ NOODLES

Squeezing rice noodles from a bag, Vân Cù, 1999

THE NEXT ROAD

H'mong women carry trays of stones to grind into pebbles that will one day ease their path to town, Hà Giang, 2009.

INTO THE WOODS

Villagers head to the forest to chop and bundle firewood to sell, Hói Mít, Lăng Cô, Thừa Thiên–Huế, 2011.

SMOKING FIELD

From ashes to fertilizer before the next planting, Hương Trà, 1999.

PART TWO From the Waters

SEASHORE SUNRISE

Shrimpers ready net at Sầm Sơn beach on the shore of the South China Sea, known in Vietnam as the East Sea (Biển Đông), September 20, 2010.

FILLING THE NET

The fisherwomen's first net is almost full, 6:28 a.m., September 20, 2010.

INSPECTION 1

A fisherwoman looks for holes in her nets as they hang drying at dawn near Đầm Cầu Hai, 2010.

BREAKFAST ON THE RIVER

Fishing families sometimes raft together to share meals. These people live on (and work from) boats about 20 feet long and under 5 feet wide: the Perfume River (Sông Hương), Huế, January, 2012.

RIVER AT DAWN

Hoping to catch small freshwater fish as they feed, this woman set out at 5 a.m. on the Như Ý river, July, 2011.

ĐÀ NĂNG MORNING

A man and three women pull a dragon net (lưới rồng), used for big fish, shortly after 7 a.m., November 25, 2010.

FISHING VESSEL

This boat, just over 30 feet long, requires many hands, Đà Nẵng beach, November, 2010.

WAITING FOR FRESH FISH

This early-bird shopper hopes for her pick of the catch, 6:04 a.m., September 28, 2010.

MOTHER NET
Fisherwomen and men empty smaller nets into the *lưới bà*; photo taken from Thuận An Bridge, Phú Vang, November, 2011.

PLENTY OF SHRIMP
Shrimp traps in a circle are a common sight in Đầm Cầu Hai, Phú Lộc, Thừa Thiên–Huế, 2010.

BOAT TIED TO DEAD TREE
People press the paddles of this wood boat with their feet to transport fish from mother nets to market, Hà Tĩnh, 2009.

GOING WITH THE FLOW
Bamboo stalks are lashed together as a raft to carry the harvester and his bounty home; this bamboo was used to make furniture, Huế, 2000.

HOUSE OF SAND
Men of Vinh Thanh commune pile sand—a common home-building material—into their buffalo carts, Huế, January, 2012.

CLEAN-UP
A visit to the shore to wash and dry nets used to cart sand, Cầu Hai Lagoon, April, 2011.

INSPECTION 2
A woman mends a billowing net at Tòa Khâm port, near the Tràng Tiền bridge, 1993.

LOOKOUT
This boy, who lives with his family in a nearby tent, guards their fenced shrimp farm, An Truyền Village, Phú An, Phú Vang, Huế, July, 2011.

THROWING THE NET
Going after small, freshwater fish on the Như Ý River, Huế, July, 2011

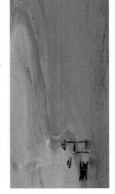

POLE FISHING
Two men on a village beach spend a spare hour pulling fish from the Lăng Cô strait; photo taken from Hải Vân mountain pass, August, 2010.

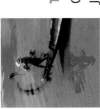

NET NUANCES
Heavy winter rains sometimes flood the Perfume River, filling it with more freshwater fish than usual. In 1999, Huế residents using homemade implements of bamboo sticks and netting, called *vó*, had very good days.

NETS ON THE PERFUME
The freshwater Perfume that runs through Huế teems with shrimp, carp and other fish, summer, 2005.

THROUGH THE BREAKERS

The locals call this 30-foot, saltwater boat a "*gọ*." Made of bamboo and wood, it's covered with asphalt, and powered by men and women with long-handle wood paddles, December, 2011.

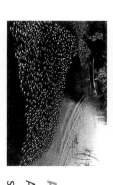

A PADDLING OF DUCKS

A farmer's son minds his family's ducks on the Nọ stream that runs by the Chợ Nọ market, Huế, 1998.

RIDING HOME

Green treasure hunters return with algae and half-sunken vegetables for their livestock, Vinh Thanh, Huế, December, 2009.

FENCE ON VINH HIỀN

A valuable bamboo fish trap (*nò sáo*) within the Tam Giang system, August, 2009.

GOLDEN NET 1

CROSSING THE TAM GIANG LAGOON

Lập An wood gatherers wade through lagoon to market their small fuel bundles, July, 2011.

GOLDEN NET 2

GOLDEN NET 3

The Golden Net series was taken from Phú Thứ Bridge, Phú Vang, Huế, July 15, 2010.

SUNSET ON LẬP AN LAGOON

Lăng Cô, April, 2011

PART THREE From the Hands of Artisans

ARTISAN

An intent woodcarver in Hương Hồ, Hương Trà, Thừa Thiên–Huế, September, 2005

YOUNG CARVER

Vietnamese renditions of the potent dragon god or god of rain go back two millennia to the *Đông Sơn* civilization; today dragon heads are used as decorative showroom or house guardians, Huế, 2000.

SHELTER FROM THE SUN

Taking shade under a large hat-umbrella, a girl embroiders wearable, bamboo-leaf hats at a crafts festival, Hai Bà Trưng schoolyard, Huế, 2005.

THREE GENERATIONS

The essential basket may catch snails, cradle spring rolls or vegetables as they steam-cook, store foods or dry goods and/or serve as covers for other baskets. Here, a boy selects bamboo straws for his grandmother to weave, after which the boy's mother makes and inserts a rim in the basket, Bao La, Quảng Điền, Thừa Thiên-Huế, August, 2007.

IN BALANCE

A bamboo basket (*thúng mủng*) crafter delivers her wares to the Bao La village market, 2009.

STREET VENDORS

Woven straw protects heads and wares from the rain, December, 2008.

FAN MAKER

This fan fashioner spreads out her traditional 17-spoke bamboo frames before covering them with rice paper, Bao La, Quảng Điền, Thừa Thiên-Huế, December, 2009.

BECOMING *BỐ ĐẠI*

A thick tree trunk is transformed into the popular statue also known as Laughing Buddha, whose identity may also derive from a folklore deity. It's said that rubbing his belly moves one closer to his contentment; Vỹ Dạ, April, 2012.

STATUES OF GODS

Bronze castings in a Thắng Lợi metal shop, Phường Đúc, 2000

AT THE FORGE

Metal smiths hammer tools from knife blades to sickles, An Cựu, 2000.

APPRENTICES

Schoolchildren devote free hours to learning a family craft, the making of *nón lá*, the traditional hat, An Lưu town, Thừa Thiên-Huế, 2005.

POETIC HATS

Mother and daughter craft "poem hats" (*nón bài thơ*) in their home. It's said they're so well-made that a poem can be seen in them. Although she is missing an arm, Ms. Thuy is well-known for her skill. Her daughter's task is attaching soft, silk strings, Huế, 2007.

MANY HATS

Milliners congregate at an early-morning market to sell their handmade hats, Dạ Lê Hat Market, 1993.

RING OF LIFE

The technology is modern but a gold (or silver) wedding necklace, to be worn with a long, silk slit dress (*áo dài*), is a traditional wedding gift from parents, Huế, 2000.

THE BRIDE

She wears her new necklace and a traditional wedding costume in good-luck red, Huế, 2012.

VILLAGE ARTIST

Some rely on local painters, such as this Chuồn villager, to create small, traditional tapestries to decorate ancestral altars during the lunar New Year (*Tết*), An Truyền, Huế, 2007.

CERAMICIST

A craftsman chisels a design in a clay vase, Thanh Lương, Phong Điền, Thừa Thiên-Huế, May, 2009.

EMBROIDERY CIRCLE

These young needlewomen, in white *áo dài* school uniforms, embroider handkerchiefs and appliqués as part of annual festival promoting classical handwork, Huế, July, 2005.

WEAVERS

Young women loom the traditional dress fabric (*xà rông*) of their high-country ethnic group (Tà ôi, Bru-Vân Kiều), Nam Đông, Phú Lộc, February, 2011.

PART FOUR Celebrating the Spirit

BOUGAINVILLEA ON BICYCLES

Townspeople wheel flowering plants home as *Tết* approaches. South American bougainvillea crossed the Atlantic with the French who later brought it to *Indochine* where the good-lunch red variety is now homegrown, Đập Đá, January, 2000.

FLOWERS IN WATER

Big bouquets of lotus for *Tết* take a freshwater drink in Tịnh Tâm lake before delivery to market, 2009.

CLEAN START

A homeowner gets ready to end one year and begin a new one, Huế, December, 2008.

STREET-SIDE SELLING

The fresh and the fabulously fake in floral arrangements meet on the side of the bridge to Cồn Hến, Huế, 2009.

SWEET SMELL OF CELEBRATION

Fragrant incense smoke wafts over *Tết* and other traditional holidays. The joss stick core is painted bamboo, on the road to Lê Ngô Cát, 2000.

BURNING BOOTS

Near year's end, many Vietnamese try to set right their relationships, including those with their ancestors. Some burn paper versions of what their ancestral spirits might need; here a woman ignites a paper hat and boots, transforming them to smoke able to enter the spirit world, Huế, 2012.

ANCESTRAL ALTAR

A woman pays her respects to the departed, An Truyền, 2011.

THE WRESTLERS

New Year festivities segued into wrestling matches metered by gong in the imperial city of Huế. Local sports fans still enjoy the choreography of two-minute bouts, Thủ Lễ, Quảng Điền, Thừa Thiên–Huế, January 29, 2012.

HEAD TO HEAD

If a wrestler is lifted off the ground by the opponent or falls to the ground, he loses. Otherwise, a village elder and a younger referee pick the winners in this one-day festival; January 29, 2012.

HERE COME THE BRIDE AND GROOM

The couple leads guests from the bride's house (where the groom has presented betel leaves and other gifts in lacquered boxes) to the groom's home, January 15, 2004.

HAND IN HAND

The bridal couple will alight at the groom's family residence for the wedding ceremony. The party will end with a marriage feast, January 15, 2004.

FESTIVE TABLE

Yellow-green areca nuts and betel leaves—signifying love and union—decorate wedding tables. Once, chewing betel (a mild but teeth-blackening stimulant, often spiced with lime) invariably started the matchmaking conversation between parents. Some country folk still chew, but among the urbane, the custom has muted into symbolism, Huế, 2012.

LIGHT THE LANTERNS

A female Buddhist nun readies lotus lanterns commemorating the Buddha's birthday, April, 2012.

LIGHTING THE NIGHT

The stacked shore lights are arranged in prayer-flag colors of blue, yellow, red, white and orange, May, 2012.

LANTERNS ON PAGODA STEPS

The Buddha is often depicted sitting on a lotus or holding this icon of ideal detachment—it floats in muddy water but is unsullied. Lotus lanterns are seen in spring on the Buddha's birthday, the eighth day of the fourth lunar month, Thiên Mụ Pagoda, March, 2008.

LANTERNS AFLOAT

The pink lotus is Vietnam's national flower; lotus lanterns float on the Perfume River under a full moon, April, 2009.

CANOPY

A worker secures paper lotuses in a canopy over Le Loi Street in Huế for the Buddha's Birthday Festival (*Lễ Phật Đản*), March, 2008.

WISHING 1

Cranes signify hope. Two small children gaze up at chains of paper cranes dangling over a pedestrian passageway, Huế, summer, 2009.

HIBISCUS IN THE MORNING

Here by day, gone by night, this rarely picked blossom may nonetheless be a key to enlightenment, May, 2012.

RED LANTERNS IN AUTUMN

Long ago, the legend goes, Chú Cuội and his wife Nguyệt Tiên climbed a magical banyan tree to the sky. Tiên slid down but the slower Cuội became the man in the moon, remembered with baked and snow-skinned (steamed) mooncakes, filled with sesame or bean paste. The red paper lanterns that illuminate the mooncake table may be released to soar, on the bank of the Perfume River, October, 2010.

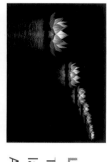

PAINTING THE ĐẦU LÂN

A teenage boy works on lion-head costumes for the children's Lion Dance of the Mooncake Festival, Huế, 1994.

LION DANCE

On a long ago autumn night, a lion saw the moon reflected in a stream and jumped in after it. Unable to capture the moon, the enraged lion charged the village but was cut down by a brave woodcutter. This epic fight is restaged during the Mooncake Festival and at other fetes, An Truyền, 2010.

SPLASH, SPLASH

The beginning of the rainy season is just another excuse for having fun, November, 2011.

GRANDMOTHER AND GRANDDAUGHTER

A Vietnamese proverb: If you want to travel fast, use the old road, Đồng Miệu Village, Phú An, Phú Vang, Thừa Thiên–Huế, 1995.

WISHING 2

A grandmother awaits a visit from her children and their children, who live far from their ancestral village, Thanh Hóa, September, 2011.

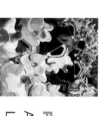

Notes on the Poetry

■ TITLE QUOTE

Sông Bạch Đằng

Núi biếc cao vút, tua tủa như gươm giáo kéo lấy tầng mây
Thuồng luồng nuốt thuỷ triều, cuộn làn sóng bạc.
Mưa xuân mới tạnh, mặt đất nở đầy bông hoa, trông như những
  cái hoa tai xinh đẹp,
Gió chiều thổi lạnh, tiếng sáo thông nổi lên rung động cả bầu trời.
Cảnh non sông xưa và nay mở đôi mắt mà xem thử,
Ngẫm lại cuộc được thua của nước Việt nước Hồ, tựa mình im
  lặng bên lan can.
Trông thấy nước dòng sông rọi bóng mặt trời buổi chiều đỏ ối,
Lầm tưởng rằng máu người chết trận vẫn chưa khô.

—Trần Minh Tông

The Bạch Đằng River

Blue peaks are swords and lances thrust at clouds.
The dragon swallows waves and spews white spray.
After spring rain, flowers deck the earth like gems—
In chilly winds, pines hum and stir the sky.
Open your eyes, admire your timeless land!
Bow and recall the strife of Viets and Huns.
Down goes the sun—the river's flowing red:
Is that the blood undried, of those war killed?

—by Trần Minh Tông, translated by Huỳnh Sanh Thông

Sông Bạch Đằng, written nearly seven centuries ago, refers to a yet earlier time when the Vietnamese repelled Chinese invaders in the region of the river. The short poem (likely composed in Chinese)—whose fifth line yields this book's title—is something of a Vietnamese anthem.

◼ PART ONE This Land that Breathes

"Trâu ơi, ta bảo trâu nầy" ("Buffalo, let me tell you something")

Trâu ơi, ta bảo trâu nầy,
Trâu ra ngoài ruộng trâu cày với ta.
Cấy cày giữ nghiệp nông gia,
Ta đây, trâu đấy, ai mà quản công?
Bao giờ cây lúa có bông,
Thì còn ngọn cỏ ngoài đồng trâu ăn.

—ca dao

The buffalo poem is one of hundreds of short, rhyming poems about daily life in the Vietnamese oral tradition known as ca dao, which developed from the 14th century (or earlier) through the 19th century. Some describe ca dao as lyrics without musical notes, because they were usually sung or chanted.

trích từ *Con Đường Quê* (*The Country Road*)

Tôi đã từng đau với nắng hè
Da tôi rạn nứt bởi khô se,
Đã từng điêu đứng khi mưa lụt
Tôi lở, thân tôi rã bốn bề.

San sẻ cùng người nỗi ấm no
Khi mùa màng được, nỗi buồn lo
Khi mùa màng mất, tôi ngày cả
Với những tình quê buổi hẹn hò.

Và thế đời tôi hết cải buồn
Trong làng. Cực khổ đằm say luôn,
Tôi thấu tê tái trong da thịt
Hương đất, hương đồng chẳng ngớt tuôn.

—Tế Hanh

Tế Hanh, born in 1921, was a poet, translator and educator. He became part of his land's New Poetry Movement in the '40s with verse that broke classical Chinese rules and expressed earthy emotion. In 1966, he won the Ho Chi Minh prize for poetry. He died in Hanoi at the age of 88.

"Ông trăng, ông trăng" (*Mr. Moon, Mr. Moon*)

Ông trăng, ông trăng,
Xuống chơi với tôi,
    Có bầu có bạn,
Có ván cơm xôi,
    Có nồi cơm nếp,
Có nệp bánh chưng,
    Có lưng hưu rượu,
Có chiếu bám du,
    Thằng cu xí xóa,
Bắt trai bỏ giỏ,
    Cái đỏ ẩm em,
Đi xem đánh cá,
    Có rá vo gạo,
Có gáo múc nước,
    Có lược chải đầu,
Có trâu cày ruộng,
    Có muống thả ao,
Ông sao trên trời

—ca dao

■ **PART TWO** From the Waters

Tâm Tình Ngư Phủ (*The Fisherman Speaks*)

Sao bằng một cõi an sanh,
Sông sâu vực thẳm, ai giành chi đây?
Sẵn dòng chèo quế một cây,
Thuyền mang một chiếc, đỡ ngày hôm mai.
Theo sông khúc vắn khúc dài,
Năm ba sợi nhợ, một vài cần tre.
Đêm trăng ngày gió, bạn bè,
Vui câu hát xướng, buồn ve rượu đào.
Thả trôi gành hạc, bãi ngao,
Thú vui non nước, mặc dầu nghinh ngang.
Cá tôm sẵn lộc trời ban,
Phận đã no đủ, còn màng của chi?. . .

—trích từ *Dương Từ Hà Mậu* của Nguyễn Đình Chiểu

Nguyễn Đình Chiểu (1822–1888) was born near Saigon, now Ho Chi Minh City. He is notable for his epic poems and his opposition to French colonial power. The fisherman's words may also be read as advice to avoid standing out in time of political unrest.

Đi Buôn (Venturing Out)

Chiều chiều vịt lội, cò bay,
Ông Voi bẻ mía chạy ngay vô rừng.
Vô rừng bứt một sợi mây;
Đem về thắt dóng cho nàng đi buôn.
Đi buôn không lỗ thì lời.
Đi ra cho thấy mặt Trời mặt Trăng.

—ca dao

Đường vô xứ Huế (The Road to Huế)

Đường vô xứ Huế quanh quanh
Non xanh nước biếc như tranh họa đồ.
Thương em, anh cũng muốn vô
Sợ Truông Nhà Hồ, sợ phá Tam Giang.

—ca dao

Đối Đáp Duyên Tình (For Two Voices)

Sông dài cá lội biệt tăm,
Phải duyên chồng vợ ngàn năm cũng chờ.
Ruộng ai thì nấy đắp bờ,
Duyên ai nấy gặp đừng chờ uổng công.

—ca dao

■ PART THREE From the Hands of Artisans

Thơ Vịnh Chiếc Nón (In Praise of the Hat)

Dáng tròn vành vạnh vốn không hư,
Che chở bao la khắp bốn bờ.
Khi để, tưởng nên dù với tán
Nên ra, thì nhạt nắng cùng mưa
Che đầu bao quản lòng tư túi,
Giúp chúa nào quên nghĩ sớm trưa.
Vòi vọi ngồi trên ngôi thượng đỉnh,
Ai ai lớn nhỏ đội ơn nhờ.

The author and date of this poem are unknown, but for centuries the widely-worn, practical conical hat also represented the ideal Confucian leader who protected and served his people, according to the poem's respected 20th-century, English-language translator Huỳnh Sanh Thông.

■ **PART FOUR** Celebrating the Spirit

trích từ **Châm** (Ode to a Sewing Needle)

Luyện tiết cứng vuỗn chẳng tà,
Khôn uốn làm câu chưa dễ nga.
Khéo léo đơn nên năm thức chỉ,
Tốt tươi thêm được bốn mùa hoa.

—Hồng Đức quốc âm thi tập

In the late 1400s, Emperor Lê Thánh Tông, championing the Vietnamese language (over Chinese), oversaw the creation of the Hồng Đức Anthology of Verse in the National Language, containing hundreds of poems by known and unknown poets. The author of this verse is unknown.

Mời Trầu (Offering Betel)

Quả cau nho nhỏ miếng trầu hôi,
Này của Xuân Hương mới quệt rồi.
Có phải duyên nhau thì thắm lại,
Đừng xanh như lá bạc như vôi.

—Hồ Xuân Hương

Hồ Xuân Hương (1772–1822) is both a great classical poet and, as a woman, an outsider poet. She is thought to have been too proud to marry.

Bông Bụt (Hibiscus)

Ánh nước hoa in một đóa hồng
Vết nhơ chẳng bén, bụt là lòng
Chiều mai nở, chiều hôm rụng
Sự lạ cho hay, tuyệt sắc không.

—Nguyễn Trãi

Nguyễn Trãi, born in 1380 in Thăng Long (now Hà Nội), saw the Ming invasion of his country, and in 1417 he joined the rebels. Nguyễn, the poet, who claimed that "it is better to conquer hearts than citadels," is considered a strategist of the successful ten-year war against Chinese occupation. After tasting court life, he retreated to his country home near an ancient Buddhist temple. Years later his wife or consort had a love affair with Vietnam's king, which ended badly in 1442 after the king died following a chat with the poet. Nguyễn, his lady and their families were executed. Two decades too late, the poet was pardoned.

Bài Ca Lưu Biệt *(A Farewell Song)*

Trăng trên trời có khi tròn khi khuyết,
Người ở đời đâu đâu khỏi tiết gian nan.
Đặng trượng phu tuỳ ngộ nhi an,
Tố hoạn nạn hành hồ hoạn nạn.
Tiền lộ định tri thiên hữu nhãn,
Thâm tiêu do hứa mộng hoàn gia,
Bấy nhiêu năm cũng vẫn chưa già.
Nọ núi Ấn, nầy sông Đà,
Non sông ấy còn chờ ta thêu dệt.
Kìa tụ tán chẳng qua là tiểu biệt,
Ngựa Tái ông họa phúc biết về đâu!
Một mai kia con tạo khéo cơ cầu,
Thấy bốn biển cũng trong vòng trời đất cả.
Ư bách niên trung tu hữu ngã,
Dẫu đến lúc núi sụp, biển lồi, trời nghiêng, đất ngả,
Tấm lòng vàng, tạc đá vẫn chưa mòn.
Trăng kia khuyết đó lại tròn.

—*Huỳnh Thúc Kháng*

Huỳnh Thúc Kháng (1876–1947) is a modern revolutionary hero; many
Vietnamese cities have streets named after him.

144

WITHDRAWN